THE ASSASSINATION OF PRESIDENT JOHN F. KENNEDY

A DAY THAT CHANGED AMERICA

by Bruce Berglund

CAPSTONE PRESS
a capstone imprint

Published by Capstone Press, an imprint of Capstone
1710 Roe Crest Drive, North Mankato, Minnesota 56003
capstonepub.com

Library of Congress Cataloging-in-Publication Data is available on the Library of Congress website.
ISBN: 9781666341683 (hardcover)
ISBN: 9781666341690 (paperback)
ISBN: 9781666341706 (ebook PDF)

Summary: John F. Kennedy was a popular American president. Not everyone stood behind him, though. On November 22, 1963, Kennedy was shot on his way to an event in Dallas, Texas. Lee Harvey Oswald waited in the Texas School Book Depository, ready to take his shot. Now readers can step back in time to learn about what led up to the assassination, how the historic event unfolded, and the ways in which one shot changed America forever.

Editorial Credits
Editor: Book Buddy Media

Consultant Credits
Richard Bell
Associate Professor of History
University of Maryland, College Park

Image Credits
Alamy: Everett Collection Historical, 7, ZUMA Press, Inc., 18; Associated Press, 13; Cecil Stoughton: White House Photographs. John F. Kennedy Presidential Library and Museum, Boston, 5, 10; Getty Images: Arnold Sachs, 6, Bettmann, 12, 21, 22, Hulton Archive, 15, Keystone-France, 20, Keystone, 26, National Archives - JFK, 24; Library of Congress, Cover, 16, 25; Robert Knudsen: White House Photographs. John F. Kennedy Presidential Library and Museum, Boston, 9; Shutterstock: amadeustx, 14, Atoly, (dots) design element throughout, Oldrich, 23, rblfmr, 19; The U.S. National Archives, 11

Source Notes
Page 8, "Ask not what your country…" John F. Kennedy, "Inaugural Address," January 20, 1961, https://www.ushistory.org/documents/ask-not.htm, Accessed December 3, 2021.

Page 13, "Mr. President, you can't say…" Report of the President's Commission on the Assassination of President John F. Kennedy, September 24, 1964, "Chapter 2: The Assassination," National Archives, https://www.archives.gov/research/jfk/warren-commission-report/chapter-2.html, Accessed December 3, 2021.

Page 15, "They are going to…" ibid.

Page 22, "I want them…" Lady Bird Johnson, "Selections from Lady Bird's Diary on the Assassination," PBS.org, November 22, 1963, https://www.pbs.org/ladybird/epicenter/epicenter_doc_diary.html, Accessed December 3, 2021.

Page 23, "This is a sad time…" Lyndon B. Johnson, "Remarks Upon Arrival at Andrews Air Force Base," November 22, 1963, https://www.presidency.ucsb.edu/documents/remarks-upon-arrival-andrews-air-force-base-0, Accessed December 3, 2021.

All internet sites appearing in back matter were available and accurate when this book was sent to press.

TABLE OF CONTENTS

Words in **bold** are in the glossary.

INTRODUCTION

On the morning of Friday, November 22, 1963, President John F. Kennedy arrived in Dallas, Texas. A limousine would take him from the airport to an event across town. The first lady, Jackie, sat next to him in the car's back seat.

It was a beautiful, sunny day. The top of the car was open. This was so people could see the Kennedys.

People lined the streets. They cheered as the president's car drove slowly through the city. Suddenly, there were gunshots. The president was hit. His car sped to the hospital. Doctors tried to save his life, but his wounds were too severe. By 1:00 that afternoon, the president was dead. His death would change the nation.

President Kennedy enjoyed talking to people and shaking their hands. He often asked his Secret Service agents to stand back.

CHAPTER 1

PRESIDENT FOR A NEW AGE

John F. Kennedy became president in 1961. Just 43 years old, he was the youngest person ever **elected** for the position. At the time, the United States was the richest country in the world. The **economy** was growing fast. New cars, televisions, and electric appliances filled people's homes.

Kennedy came from a family of politicians and businesspeople. To many, he represented American values.

But there were also problems. Many people feared war could start between the United States and its rival, the Soviet Union. At home, Black Americans were treated like second-class citizens. When they **protested** for their rights, there were violent attacks by white people.

Kennedy met with civil rights leaders, including Martin Luther King Jr. (second from left) on August 28, 1963.

FACT

In 1957, the Soviet Union launched the first satellite into space. In 1961, the country had its first astronaut. Many Americans felt the United States was falling behind in exploring space.

Faced with these problems, Kennedy wanted to inspire Americans. His speeches were positive and hopeful. He believed people should serve their nation. When he became president, he stated, "Ask not what your country can do for you—ask what you can do for your country."

As president, Kennedy started the Peace Corps. This program sent young Americans to other countries. There, they worked in schools and clinics. Kennedy vowed that the United States would land an astronaut on the moon before the end of the 1960s. He asked for more rights for Black Americans.

Many people loved the Kennedys. First Lady Jackie was elegant and popular. Her picture was often in magazines. People watched her on TV. The Kennedys had two small children, Caroline and John Jr. They seemed like the perfect family.

People across the nation admired their president. Many Americans believed in his inspiring speeches. They thought that the 1960s would bring great things for the United States. They expected Kennedy would lead the nation for years to come.

John F. Kennedy holds John Jr. as Jackie holds Caroline.

CHAPTER 2

TRAGEDY IN DALLAS

When the Kennedys visited Dallas, the 1964 presidential election was a year away. President Kennedy hoped he could convince the people of Texas to vote for him.

The Kennedys planned to spend two days in Texas. They would visit five cities.

When Air Force One landed in Dallas, hundreds of people were waiting at the airport. Jackie was the first to come out of the plane. Her pink two-piece suit was bright in the sunshine. The crowd cheered. Her husband followed behind. People waved flags, took photos, and held homemade signs.

> **FACT**
> Presidents travel in a plane called Air Force One. It has an office and a bedroom for the president. There is also space for all the president's assistants.

Jackie's pink suit was one of her favorites. The trip to Dallas was the seventh time she wore it.

The governor of Texas, John Connally, sat in a place of honor. He and his wife rode with the Kennedys in the limousine. A **motorcade** of more than 30 cars and motorcycles surrounded them. The Secret Service agents who guarded the president were in the car right behind his. The other cars held Vice President Lyndon B. Johnson, members of Congress, U.S. Army generals, and the mayor of Dallas. Police officers and reporters were there too.

The president's limousine had a special seat that could be raised as high as 10.5 inches (26.7 centimeters). This gave people a better view of the car's passengers.

Thousands of people lined the streets. Twice, Kennedy's car stopped. Kennedy shook hands with people. He also took the time to talk to a group of children.

"Mr. President, you can't say Dallas doesn't love you," said the governor's wife.

Kennedy smiled.

President Kennedy liked being up close and personal with people.

At about 12:30, the motorcade turned a corner at Dealey Plaza. The open limousine passed slowly in front of a tall brick building, the Texas School Book **Depository**. On the sixth floor, a man aimed a rifle out an open window. His name was Lee Harvey Oswald.

The Texas School Book Depository stored and shipped out school textbooks.

It is believed that Oswald sat at this window on the sixth floor of the Texas School Book Depository.

Oswald fired. The bullet missed the car. Some people who heard the noise thought it was from a motorcycle engine. But other people knew right away it was a gunshot.

Oswald fired again. The second shot hit the president in the upper back. The bullet also hit Governor Connally.

"They are going to kill us all!" the governor shouted. The limousine sped up.

An aerial view of Dealey Plaza; the Texas School Book Depository is to the left.

Kennedy clutched at the wound in his neck. Jackie leaned over to help. A Secret Service agent started running to the president's car. Oswald fired again. The shot rang out just as the Secret Service agent reached the car.

Oswald's third shot hit the president in the head. Kennedy slumped over in his seat. Jackie screamed. The Secret Service agent pushed her into the back seat and protected her in case the shooter fired again. The motorcade raced to the hospital.

On the sixth floor of the Texas School Book Depository, Oswald hid the rifle behind some boxes. Then he walked to the stairs.

CHAPTER 3

DEATH OF THE PRESIDENT

Doctors rushed President Kennedy into the emergency room. He was barely breathing. Then, his heart stopped. Jackie, standing by in her bloody pink dress and jacket, waited for news. At 1:00, the doctors let her know that her husband was dead.

Jackie removed her hat and white gloves at the hospital. They were lost and have never been found. The real pink suit is in the National Archives and won't be displayed until at least 2100. Replicas have been made to display.

By that time, radio and television stations were already reporting that the president had been shot. Journalists waited at the hospital for updates. The White House waited 30 minutes to share the news.

The Dallas Morning News was the first newspaper to break the news of Kennedy's assassination.

FACT

The bullet that hit Governor Connally passed through his shoulder. It broke his wrist before stopping in his thigh. Doctors operated on Connally for four hours. His wounds were severe, but he survived.

Vice President Johnson feared his life was at risk too. As soon as he learned Kennedy was dead, Johnson sneaked out of the hospital with Secret Service agents. He went to the airport. He would be safe on Air Force One.

Soon after, the casket carrying the president's body arrived at the airport. Jackie watched as it was loaded on Air Force One. Meanwhile, Johnson was preparing to be sworn in as the new president. He asked Jackie if she would stand with him as he said the **oath**. She stood on his left. His wife, Lady Bird, stood on his right.

The president's body was flown back to Andrews Air Force Base in Washington, D.C.

FROM VICE PRESIDENT TO PRESIDENT

If the president dies in office, the vice president takes their place. As soon as Kennedy's death was announced, Johnson automatically became president. Still, he wanted to take the oath before Air Force One left Dallas. He wanted it to be official. Jackie knew it was important to show the nation that she supported him.

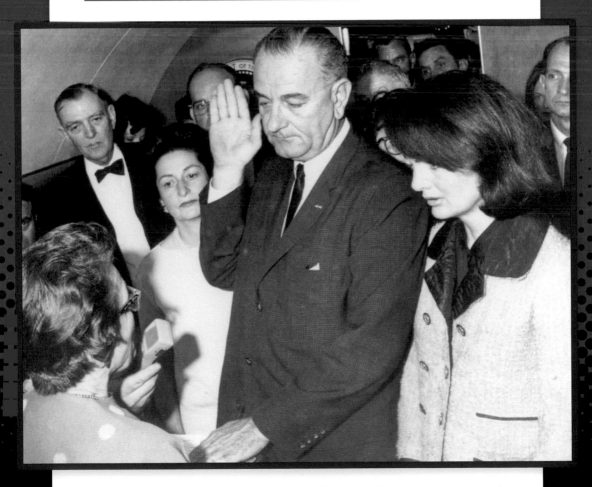

from left: Lady Bird Johnson, Lyndon B. Johnson, Jackie Kennedy

After President Johnson was sworn in, Air Force One took off. People across the country watched live on television as the plane arrived in Washington, D.C. The president's casket was lowered and carried to an ambulance. Jackie remained by her husband's side. She was still wearing the bloodstained suit. When someone asked if she wanted to change her clothes, she said no. "I want them to see what they have done," she said.

Mourners gathered outside Parkland Hospital in Dallas after receiving news of the president's death.

The United States Postal Service released a stamp on May 29, 1964, President Kennedy's birthday.

President Johnson spoke to the nation from the airport. He said, "This is a sad time for all people. We have suffered a loss that cannot be weighed . . . I will do my best. That is all I can do."

CHAPTER 4

CATCHING THE KILLER

Lee Harvey Oswald was stopped as he tried to leave the Texas School Book Depository. An armed police officer stood before him.

Oswald's boss told the officer that Oswald was an employee. It was true. Oswald had worked there for about a month. The two men rushed past Oswald.

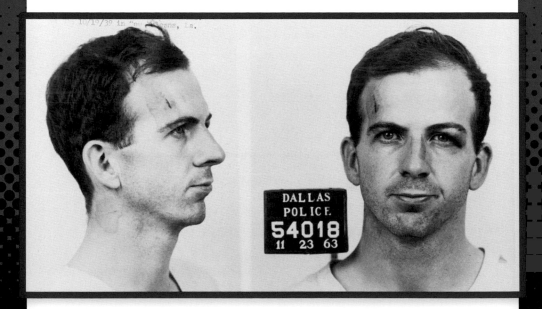

Oswald was angry at America. He thought that killing Kennedy would send a message to the country.

But Oswald wasn't free for long. Workers quickly noticed their coworker was gone. Then police found the rifle. Records showed that Oswald was the owner. As Oswald waited for a bus, another officer approached him. Oswald shot the officer and hid in a movie theater. Just over an hour after he had shot the president, Oswald was arrested.

Two days after Kennedy's **assassination**, Oswald was being moved from the police station to jail. On the way, a man named Jack Ruby shot and killed Oswald. Ruby said he didn't want Jackie Kennedy to watch her husband's killer on trial.

Jack Ruby (right) shot and killed Oswald (center) in the basement of the police station.

CHAPTER 5

A NATION MOURNS

The president's funeral was held on Monday, November 25. After the church service, a horse-drawn carriage brought his coffin across the Potomac River to Arlington National Cemetery. As the carriage drove by, John Jr. saluted. For many people, the little boy saluting his father symbolized the president's service to the country.

Kennedy's coffin rested in the Capitol rotunda on November 24. More than 250,000 people came to pay their respects. The next day, he was buried.

MOURNING TOGETHER

Kennedy's assassination was one of the first major events of the media age. For the first time, people could watch the news as it happened, live on television. People across the country heard news of the president's shooting minutes after it happened. Millions of people watched his funeral live on television. The Kennedy assassination was a tragic event that Americans experienced together, at the same time, through media.

For many years, people wondered if history would be different if Kennedy had lived. By the end of the 1960s, the United States was involved in a difficult war in Vietnam. Conflicts between the police and people fighting for their rights increased. In April 1968, Martin Luther King Jr. was assassinated. Robert Kennedy was assassinated in June. Robert was John's younger brother. He was also a popular politician. For many people, the hope they felt when John F. Kennedy was elected was gone.

On June 24, 1970, the John F. Kennedy Memorial Plaza was opened in Dallas. It stands a block away from Dealey Plaza. It is meant to symbolize the freedom of the president's spirit. Thousands of people visit the memorial every year.

TIMELINE

NOVEMBER 8, 1960: John F. Kennedy is elected president of the United States.

OCTOBER 15, 1963: Lee Harvey Oswald applies for a job at the Texas School Book Depository.

NOVEMBER 21, 1963: The Kennedys leave for a five-city, two-day visit to Texas. They stop in San Antonio first, then spend the night in Fort Worth.

NOVEMBER 22, 1963

8:45 A.M.: Kennedy greets crowds in the parking lot of his hotel in Fort Worth.

9:25 A.M.: Kennedy delivers his last public speech.

11:38 A.M.: Air Force One lands at Love Field in Dallas.

11:52 A.M.: The motorcade leaves Love Field.

12:30 P.M.: Oswald shoots Kennedy and Governor Connally as the motorcade drives through Dealey Plaza.

12:36 P.M.: Kennedy arrives at the hospital; he is pronounced dead at 1 p.m.

1:22 P.M.: Oswald's rifle is discovered; Oswald is captured at 1:50 p.m.

2:38 P.M.: Lyndon B. Johnson takes the oath of office.

NOVEMBER 23, 1963: Oswald is charged with murdering Kennedy. President Johnson proclaims November 25, the day of Kennedy's funeral, as a national day of mourning.

NOVEMBER 24, 1963

11:21 A.M.: Jack Ruby shoots Oswald. Oswald is pronounced dead at 1:07 p.m.

12:08 P.M.: Kennedy's memorial service begins at the U.S. Capitol.

NOVEMBER 25, 1963: Kennedy is buried at Arlington National Cemetery.

JUNE 24, 1970: The John F. Kennedy Memorial Plaza is dedicated.

GLOSSARY

assassination (uh-sass-uh-NAY-shun)—the murder of someone who is well known or important

depository (di-PAH-zuh-tor-ee)—a place where things are stored

economy (i-KAH-nuh-mee)—the ways in which a country handles its money and resources

elect (ih-LEKT)—to choose a leader by voting

motorcade (MOH-tur-kayd)—group of cars or other motorized vehicles traveling together

oath (OHTH)—a serious, formal promise

protest (pro-TEST)—to object to something strongly and publicly

READ MORE

Koestler-Grack, Rachel A. *John F. Kennedy.* Minneapolis: Bellwether Media, Inc., 2022.

Markovics, Joyce L. *1969 Vietnam War Protest March.* Ann Arbor, MI: Cherry Lake Publishing, 2021.

Shanté, Angela. *The Movement: 1963.* New York: Franklin Watts, an imprint of Scholastic Inc., 2022.

INTERNET SITES

35th President—John F. Kennedy
c-span.org/series/?presidents&pres=35

John F. Kennedy Facts for Kids
kids.kiddle.co/John_F._Kennedy

The White House: John F. Kennedy
whitehouse.gov/about-the-white-house/presidents/john-f-kennedy/

INDEX

Author Biography

Bruce Berglund was a history professor for 19 years. He taught courses on ancient and modern history, war and society, women's history, and sports history. Bruce was a Fulbright Scholar three times, and he has traveled to 16 different countries in Europe and Asia for research and teaching.